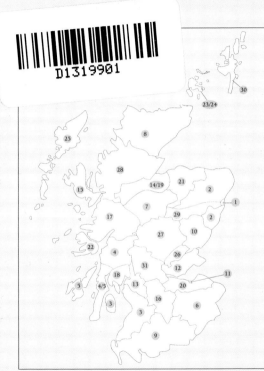

1. Aberdeen
2. Aberdeenshire
3. Arran & Ayrshire
4. Argyll
5. Southern Argyll
6. The Borders
7. The Cairngorms
8. Caithness & Sutherland
9. Dumfries and Galloway
10. Dundee & Angus
11. Edinburgh
12. Fife, Kinross & Clackmannan
13. Glasgow
14. Inverness
15. The Isle of Skye
16. Lanarkshire

17. Lochaber
18. Loch Lomond, Cowal & Bute
19. Loch Ness
20. The Lothians
21. Moray
22. Mull & Iona
23. Orkney
24. Orkney in Wartime
25. The Outer Hebrides
26. The City of Perth
27. Highland Perthshire
28. Ross & Cromarty
29. Royal Deeside
30. Shetland
31. Stirling & The Trossachs

The remaining four books, Caledonia, Distinguished Distilleries, Scotland's Mountains and Scotland's Wildlife feature locations throughout the country so are not included in the above list.

SHETLAND

COLIN NUTT
Author and photographer

lyricalscotland

2 St Ninian's Isle lies just off the west coast of southern Mainland near the village of Bigton.
At low tide it is joined to the mainland by this wonderful double-sided 'tombolo' beach.

SHETLAND

Welcome to Shetland!

People have lived in Shetland for up to six thousand years, the earliest of them being Neolithic farmers. So it seems appropriate to be welcomed to the islands by this woman whose face has been reconstructed from her skull by the wonders of modern technology. See how the folk of those days were very similar to us! Indeed, her descendants may still be living in Shetland to this day. The population of which she may be an ancestor today numbers 22,500, about 7,500 of whom live in Lerwick, Shetland's capital.

Given Shetland's history, the question of how Scottish it is bears asking. Before the Viking (or Norse) invasions that began around 800AD, it's clear that Shetland, like much of (what would become) Scotland, was part of the Pictish culture, so there was common cause until then. But the Vikings' arrival led to Shetland eventually becoming the northern third of the great earldom that was based in Orkney during the Norse/Viking golden age. As Shetland remained part of the Norse empire until 1468, it was a Norse land for around 650 years, whereas it has been Scottish for only the last 540 or so years. So while today it is of course well and truly part of Scotland, it retains an 'other-worldly' feel as a result of its Norse period which expresses itself in many place-names and aspects of its culture. Perhaps the most high profile Norse-related event

Held annually on the last Tuesday in January, the Lerwick Up Helly Aa festival started in the 1880s but relates to the years of Norse sovereignty. The climax is the burning of the galley.

is the fire festival of Up Helly Aa, held in January at many places in Shetland.

Shetland is a Treasure Trove of archaeology. Secrets of its ancient past can be found at Jarlshof and Old Scatness Village, both at the southern tip of Shetland near Sumburgh Airport. Jarlshof presents a history of almost uninterrupted habitation from around 2500BC to the 1600sAD. Here, the evolution of architectural style and practice can be charted from the Neolithic Age through the Bronze Age, Iron Age, Norse and Medieval periods. (See right and pages 8-11)

Shetland is, of course, the most northerly part of Scotland and thus the British Isles: the 60° north line of latitude passes through the southern part of Shetland's Mainland. This puts it on a level with the southern tip of Greenland! And it is closer to Bergen in Norway than it is to Edinburgh. During the Second World War, Shetland's proximity to Norway and its historical links led to the setting up of a supply line, initially using fishing boats to ship arms, ammunition and other supplies to occupied Norway.

6   A close look at some of the intricate stonework at Jarlshof.

Returning boats brought out refugees and those fleeing the Gestapo. This service was nicknamed the 'Shetland Bus' – see also pp.23 & 63. The Shetland archipelago is extensive, stretching about 100 miles from Fair Isle in the south (see pictures on pp.1 & 96) to Muckle Flugga in the north. It comprises over 100 islands, 15 of which are inhabited.

This book is set out in the form of a guided tour around the Shetland Isles, beginning in the south and working northwards. On the way, we take in many islands and the more remote areas of Shetland's Mainland. The isles of Mousa, Burra, Bressay, Noss, Foula, Papa Stour, Whalsay, Yell, Fetlar, Unst and Muckle Flugga all show off their differing characters and unique charms. Along the way, many of Shetland's birds and animals make an appearance, from ponies to puffins and sheep to skuas. All in all, a journey of immense variety and considerable drama lies ahead . . .

Period reconstruction of a crofthouse at the Shetland Museum in Lerwick.

8 This view of Jarlshof gives an idea of the extensive nature of the site. Looking south, in the foreground on the left are remains of the Norse settlement developed in the 800s.

To the right of this is the location of the wheelhouses (see over), behind which stands the hall built in the 1580s by Earl Robert Stewart. Sumburgh Head is in the distance. 9

10 Parts of four wheelhouses from the 2nd and 3rd centuries survive at Jarlshof. One of them – the circular grass-roofed structure – is built into the courtyard of the Iron-Age broch.

This is the Iron-Age broch at Old Scatness, dating from 400 – 200BC, which would have been much taller when built (see Mousa broch on p.18). Fitful Head stands in the distance.

12 Moving a few miles north to Dunrossness, the Crofthouse Museum is a mid-19th century Shetland
croft which was lived in until the late 1960s. Such houses evolved over many centuries and were

well adapted to stand up to Shetland's sometimes fierce weather. Open to the public, this example 13
has been superbly restored with the above room setting reflecting the 1880s.

14 On the western side of Dunrossness, Quendale Water Mill has been refurbished to the highest standard and is a wonderful example of Shetland's industrial heritage.

Shetland ponies are understandably famous throughout the world. These gorgeous specimens are at **15** Gue Stud in Dunrossness, but ponies can be seen all over the Shetland Isles.

16 Shetland is also renowned for its huge and varied seabird colonies. Guillemots are among the 21 species which breed in Shetland. Over a million seabirds return here every summer to breed.

The road north from Quendale leads to the lovely Loch of Spiggie, which hosts an RSPB reserve. 17
The sea, never far away in Shetland, can be seen in the distance.

18 The island of Mousa, off the east coast of southern Shetland, boasts the tallest surviving broch anywhere! The cormorant seems keen to point it out. Inset: Arctic terns breed here in summer.

Inside the broch it is possible to gain a better idea of the complexity of these double-walled structures. Some of the openings lead through to the cavity between the inner and outer walls.

20 Moods of Shetland 1: the islands often feel the force of North Atlantic storms on their western coasts. Here, a westerly gale causes the sea to batter the island of West Burra.

Mood 2: Shetland is not greatly affected by snow, but when it does settle it provides some **21** spectacular views, such as here at Scalloway on the west coast. Foula lies on the horizon.

22 Mood 3: Again at Scalloway, this glorious evening scene across the East Voe (bay) shows Shetland light at its beautiful best.

KNM Hitra visits Scalloway to celebrate the 70th anniversary of her donation by the USA to replace 23
the Norwegian fishing boats on 'Shetland Bus' missions to supply the Norwegian resistance.

24 Located on the west coast, Scalloway is Shetland's second-largest settlement after Lerwick and until 1708 was its capital. The 1600-built castle, just right of centre, was the residence of the much-loathed

Earl Patrick Stewart, designed to flaunt his wealth and intimidate his enemies. The modern building to its right is Scalloway Museum. The busy harbour is the base for an active fishing fleet.

26 Now it's time to make the six-mile journey across to the east coast and explore Lerwick, Shetland's capital and only town. This view, taken from an arriving ferry, looks towards the centre.

The old harbour remains active with smaller vessels and some cruise ships. In the foreground is a **27** replica Norse longboat and beyond, the ferry to Bressay is ready to depart.

28 This night view shows the other side of the old harbour. The building to the right of centre with a clock tower is the RNLI office. Lerwick was a major player in the days of the herring boom.

This is the part of Lerwick known as Lodberries, a collective name for the old houses, stores and 29 piers that line the shore. The name comes from the Norse 'hlad berg' meaning flat stone.

30 Fort Charlotte was built in the 17th century to defend the town from the Dutch, who later destroyed it. Reconstructed in 1782, it is named after the wife of King George III.

Shetland Museum & Archives is located at Hay's Dock, seen here, which also forms an exterior area **31** of the Museum. The vintage boat on the right is one of the exhibits.

32 Clickimin Broch sits on the shores of a lochan in south Lerwick and is a good example of a broch tower with associated secondary buildings constructed in the Iron Age.

The island of Bressay is a short ferry crossing from Lerwick. The 122m/400ft Ord cliffs at its
southern end are seen here as evening cloud rises to engulf them, all in all a dramatic sight.

34 Next to Bressay Heritage Centre is this Bronze Age burnt mound. Such sites are where stones were roasted in fire then dropped in water to raise the temperature, but for what purpose is not clear.

Left: the 'Noss Boat' takes visitors on wildlife tours around the islands of Bressay and Noss. **35**
Right: Shetland's parliament met on this small promontory on Tingwall Loch until the late 1500s.

36 Nesbister Böd stands on the lovely inlet of Whiteness Voe near Tingwall. In Shetland, a Böd was a building used to house fishermen and their gear during the fishing season.

Now we are in West Mainland, at Neolithic Staneydale 'Temple'. It is so named because it might have been a place of worship, or it may have been a chieftain's house or community hall.

38 Continuing westwards, the village of Walls nestles at the head of Vaila Sound and has a well-sheltered harbour. As the sun sets, a local fishing boat sets off towards the open sea.

The village of Melby is at the end of the road through West Mainland. Evening light sends long shadows across St Margaret's kirkyard. On the horizon lies Papa Stour, our next destination. **39**

40 But first, another look at the Whiteness area, specifically the wonderful panoramic view to be enjoyed from the road between there and Tingwall. The peninsula in the lower half of the picture is so typically

Shetland with its scattered settlements, once mainly a crofting landscape. Distant islands and skerries **41** stir the imagination.

42 Papa Stour is packed with points of interest, but small enough to walk around most of it during the course of a day trip. Here at Hamna Voe, shelters have been made to protect the boats.

Left: near the head of Hamna Voe are these two partially restored Norse-era watermills. 43
Right: the channel that takes the water from one to the other includes a mini aqueduct.

44 Aisha Head on the west coast of Papa Stour is perhaps the most spectacular part of a generally impressive coastline. Behind the headland are Fugla Skerry (left) and Leera Skerry.

Looking through the natural arch of Aisha Head reveals another, smaller, arch in the base of Leera **45**
Skerry. At the time of writing it is quite safe to cross Aisha Head arch, which opens up

46 further fine views such as this huge stack named 'Da Snolda'. Right: a little to the south is Kirstan's Hole, a collapsed inland cavern reached by the sea through the cave at the end.

Foula is a most alluring island, perhaps because it is distant yet visible from many places in Shetland **47** (p.21 for example). Papa Stour is closer and provides a better idea of its rugged nature.

Da Sneck o'
da Smaallie

48 Lying about 20 miles west of Walls, it is one the most remote of Scotland's islands. It supports a population of about 30, some of whom live here in Hametoun. Inset: improvised signpost.

And the subject of that signpost? Da Sneck o da Smaallie is a remarkable rock fault 30m/98ft deep. **49**
The left-hand view shows its setting while on the right we see into the dank, treacherous interior.

50 This aerial picture shows the western tip of Foula and gives a good idea of the extent to which the cliff is undercut at sea level. This is an island of magnificent cliffs, the highest being Da Kame,

Inset sign text:

AIRSTRIP
PAYPHONE
TOILETS

at 376m/1233ft one of the highest in Britain. Pictured here is the jagged and fractured north coast **51** with the Garda Stack near the top, its arch quite easily seen. Inset: self explanatory!

52 Shetland wool is a significant part of the economy and comes from many breeds of sheep. These four characters were all spotted on Foula, but sheep are farmed throughout the islands.

Now back on West Mainland and heading north by Aith Voe, a walk of a few minutes up the **53** Lunklet Burn is rewarded by the sight of this fine waterfall.

54 In the maritime landscape of Shetland, harbours and piers are everywhere and always add interest. This one is at the village of Voe, situated at the head of Olna Firth.

Although Olna Firth is on the west side of Shetland, only a few miles further on Dury Voe is on the **55** eastern coast. On a mellow morning, this view greets those waiting for the ferry to Whalsay.

56 But before the next island odyssey, a 'taster' of what lies further north. Returning to the road just travelled, at a point between Lunklet Burn and Voe, this grand scene surveys the Gon Firth,

complete with fish farms, and looks north towards Busta Voe and the village of Brae. On the left side **57** of the horizon is Ronas Hill, the highest point in Shetland at 450m/1476ft.

58 And so to Symbister on Whalsay, where 17th-century trading links with northern Europe via
the Hanseatic League are recalled by the picturesque Pier House. Symbister is one of Shetland's

principal fishing ports and home to some of Europe's largest fishing vessels, some of which can be seen in the background of the picture opposite. Here though is something a little more modest.

60 Whalsay is quite populous for its size, with a community of over 1,000. The village of Brough is on its north coast and pleasingly typifies Shetland's spacious settlements.

With the great majority of its trees long gone, peat remains a significant source of fuel on Shetland. **61**
Cut peat requires many weeks to dry and careful stacking aids the process.

62 Whalsay Parish Church stands on this promontory on the edge of Brough and is somewhat mirrored by the grass-roofed barn. Beyond lies the Mainland district of Lunna, our next destination.

Lunna House originates from 1663 but its main claim to fame is as the original headquarters of what came to be known as the 'Shetland Bus' operations to support Norwegian resistance in WW2.

64 Lunna Kirk with its lovely, if compact, interior and gallery on three sides is the oldest working church in Shetland, with origins that probably go back to the 12th century.

The road to the north passes through the large village of Brae, the last settlement of any size in these **65** parts. Its amenities and pleasant setting make it a good base from which to explore.

66 The western seaboard of North Mainland presents the greatest concentration of stunning coastal scenery in Shetland. The cliffs and stacks at the Ness of Hillswick are examples of this.

Perhaps most striking of all is this skeletal rocky remnant that hints at the extent of the land in **67** former times. Known as The Drongs, it is pictured from Tangwick. PS: spot the rabbit?

68 From a different angle The Drongs present a slightly different profile and a wonderful silhouette at sunset.

Tangwick Haa Museum in Eshaness preserves the history of the area in the setting of an historic **69** house. Seen here is the Laird's Room as it would have been in the late 19th/early 20th century.

70 The islet of Dore Holm off Eshaness boasts what must be one of the biggest natural arches in Shetland. From land it is best seen from Tangwick, but being viewed by boat must be even better.

Seldom pictured due to their remote location on the west coast of North Roe (the most northerly district of Mainland), Lang Clodie Loch Falls are the highest in Shetland and drop into the sea.

72 This panoramic view of the famously dramatic Eshaness cliffs gives an idea of the scale of the landscape thanks to the people on the cliff top. The thought of the sea crashing right over the full

height of these basalt lava cliffs is awe-inspiring. On stormy days it is dangerous to go anywhere near the cliff edge as sizeable rocks can be thrown up by the sea.

74 Here at the Uyea coastline, North Roe, are the oldest rocks in Shetland, Lewisian gneiss formed almost three billion years ago. Getting here requires a four-mile walk from North Roe village.

Uyea island is tidal, connected to the mainland at low tide by this sandbar. This is a pupping ground for grey seals and among this group are a few youngsters born earlier in the year.

76 Now we move from the land at the top of this picture to the island of Yell, second largest in Shetland after Mainland. Crofthouses, past and present, can be seen in this view at Ness of Sound.

You never know what wildlife surprises Shetland will present you with. This bearded seal (check out those whiskers!) is a rare visitor from the Arctic, basking at Sellafirth, Yell.

FROM GLOUP
SIXERN ELIZA

78 Left: a study in drystone walling at Gloup in the north of Yell. Right: memorial to the Gloup disaster of 1881 when a storm caused the loss of 10 fishing boats and 58 men.

Boarding ferries is as much a part of life in Shetland as getting into a car. From Gutcher, at the north end of Yell, ferries cross to the islands of Fetlar and Unst.

80 And on Fetlar near the ferry pier is 19th-century Brough Lodge, in the grounds of which stands this imposing yet merely ornamental tower, built on the site of an Iron Age broch.

Glorious beaches abound in Shetland, such as Tresta beach at the head of Wick of Houbie on 81
Fetlar's southern coast. Fetlar's population is currently around 80; in 1836 it was 860.

82 Fetlar is known as the 'Garden of Shetland' due to it being the greenest of all the islands. Hints of its fertility can be seen here in the hay harvest. Papil Loch lies beyond the chapel.

Fetlar was very badly affected by the 'Clearances' which reduced its population by over a third **83** in 25 years – one reason for deserted buildings like this. Inset: flowers of the field.

84 An idyllic coastal nook in the Wick of Gruiting on the north side of Fetlar. On the horizon, more land can just be made out: this is Unst, our final and most northerly destination.

And at the south-eastern corner of Unst stands Muness Castle, built by Laurence Bruce from 1598. **85**
Of Z-plan design and originally of three storeys, it has circular towers at opposing corners.

86 On the other side of Unst, St Olaf's Norse-era church enjoys a beautiful setting overlooking Lunda Wick and its white-sand beach. Inset: Lund standing stone, one of many in Shetland.

Moving north, this is Baltasound harbour. Almost everywhere in Shetland exudes a feeling of **87** spaciousness, often enhanced by wonderful light; this evening scene captures something of that.

88 The north of Unst is marked by two substantial hills, the higher and more prominent of which is Saxa Vord, at 285m/935ft the highest point in Unst. Naturally, it is a great viewpoint and provides

this evening image looking south down Burra Firth and the Loch of Cliff. The sun has gone down and the mist is coming up, yet it's quite light for 9.45pm – but that's what you get this far north.

90 Back in Baltasound, every visitor has to see what is possibly the world's most famous bus shelter! It has been lovingly embellished since being built and even has its own website.

Unst Boat Haven in Haroldswick is a brilliantly presented museum as this picture goes some way to **91** showing. It harbours some fine original boats that have been in use over the past 140 years.

92 The other hill at the north of Unst is Hermaness. You wouldn't know it from this picture, but the best thing about Hermaness is that it's the summer home of thousands of puffins!

These delightful birds have no fear of humans and come to greet you! Their possible comments, **93** clockwise from top left: 'Is this my good side?'; 'I'm a bit shy'; 'Look out!'; 'I like these flowers'.

94 Shetland has a wealth of other seabirds so here are a few more. Clockwise from top left: great skua, known locally as the 'bonxie' (puffins beware); gannet; fulmar; oystercatcher.

And so we reach journey's end: Hermaness is also the best place from which to see Muckle Flugga, **95** the most northerly island in the British Isles. The back cover picture shows the lighthouse.

Published 2017 by Lyrical Scotland, an imprint of Lomond Books Ltd, Broxburn, EH52 5NF
www.lyricalscotland.com www.lomondbooks.com

Originated by Ness Publishing, 47 Academy Street, Elgin, Moray, IV30 1LR
(Published 2014, reprinted 2015 & 2016 by Ness Publishing)

Printed in China

All photographs © Colin and Eithne Nutt except p.1 © Undiscovered Scotland; p.5 © John Coutts;
p.14 © Geordie Jacobson; p.15 top left, top right & lower right © Carole Laignel;
pp.20-23 and pp.68 & 71 © William Moore; p.35 (left) © Georges Dif; p.96 © Ed Tooth

Text © Colin Nutt
ISBN 978-1-78818-011-5

Front cover: puffins at Hermaness; p.1: South Haven and Sheep Rock, Fair Isle;
p.4: Neolithic woman modelled at Shetland Museum, Lerwick; this page: Fair Isle, with the Bird Observatory
visible towards the right; back cover: Muckle Flugga lighthouse

While the Publisher endeavours to ensure the accuracy of information provided, no responsibility
can be taken for errors or omissions. The publisher welcomes information should any be found.